EMMANUEL JOSEPH

The Mythic Match, How Artificial Intelligence and Legendary Stories Shape Modern Athletics

Contents

1

Chapter 1: The Genesis of AI in Athletics

Athletic training has always been a science, but with the advent of artificial intelligence (AI), it has become an exact one. Imagine a world where a runner's stride is analyzed to the millisecond, optimizing every footfall for speed and efficiency. This transformation wasn't instantaneous—it started with basic data analytics and wearable technology, growing increasingly sophisticated with machine learning algorithms that can predict injury risks and personalize training regimens.

Yet, the application of AI extends far beyond physical conditioning. It's in the strategic planning that goes into every play of a football match, the predictive models that foresee an opponent's next move, and the virtual reality simulations that place athletes in high-pressure scenarios to improve mental fortitude. These technologies have become indispensable, shaping a new generation of athletes who are not just fit but smart.

It's essential to trace the origins of AI's incorporation into sports to appreciate its impact fully. The journey began modestly, with motion sensors and heart rate monitors, leading up to today's sophisticated predictive analytics and biomechanical assessments. From monitoring hydration levels to preventing concussions, AI's role is ever-evolving and ever-expanding, cementing its place as a cornerstone of modern athletics.

The mythology here is not one of gods and monsters but one of human ingenuity and technological advancement. AI, once the stuff of science fiction, has taken its place as a true game-changer in the athletic realm, rewriting the rules and setting new standards for excellence and safety.

2

Chapter 2: The Legendary Roots of Modern Sports

Long before AI entered the arena, sports were intertwined with mythology and legend. The ancient Greeks viewed their athletes as heroes, with the Olympic Games serving as a stage for epic displays of strength and skill. Each competition was more than just a physical test; it was a homage to the gods, a demonstration of the human spirit's potential.

Legends like Achilles and Hercules were the early archetypes of athletic prowess. Their stories were passed down through generations, each tale imbued with lessons on courage, endurance, and the relentless pursuit of greatness. These mythic narratives shaped the very fabric of early sports, where victory was not just an achievement but a testament to one's character and favor with the divine.

In medieval Europe, tournaments and jousts took on a similarly mythical aura. Knights competed for honor and glory, their feats becoming the stuff of legend. The very concept of chivalry and valor was deeply rooted in these athletic endeavors, reinforcing societal ideals and inspiring generations to come.

Today, these legendary roots still influence modern sports. The narratives of past heroes echo in the present, reminding us that sports are more than just games. They are arenas where human potential is realized and celebrated, where the echoes of mythical stories still resonate, guiding and inspiring athletes in their quests for greatness.

3

Chapter 3: The Intersection of Myth and Technology

The convergence of ancient myth and modern technology in sports is nothing short of fascinating. In many ways, AI has become the modern counterpart to the gods of old, possessing an omnipotence that can dictate the outcome of games and shape the future of athletes. Just as the ancients believed in the gods' direct influence on their lives, today's athletes trust AI to guide them towards excellence.

This intersection can be seen in the way AI helps athletes harness their "inner hero." Technologies such as augmented reality bring mythic training scenarios to life, allowing athletes to train as if they were legendary warriors. Biomechanical analysis reveals the weaknesses and strengths of their "Achilles' heel," offering paths to overcoming them.

Moreover, AI has brought a level of precision to sports that parallels the mythic ideals of perfection and heroism. Data analytics create a near-omniscient view of an athlete's performance, while machine learning algorithms provide insights that seem almost prophetic. It's as if the wisdom of the ages has been encoded into these systems, offering guidance and support to athletes at every turn.

The mythical and the technological thus coexist harmoniously, each enhancing the other. The myths provide the narrative framework that inspires and motivates, while AI offers the tools and insights needed to achieve those mythic ideals. Together, they forge a new era of athletics, where the past and future come together to shape the present.

4

Chapter 4: AI as the Modern-Day Oracle

In the ancient world, oracles were revered for their ability to predict the future and offer divine guidance. Today, AI serves a similar role in athletics, using data and algorithms to foresee outcomes and provide strategic insights. The predictive capabilities of AI are nothing short of miraculous, offering athletes and coaches a glimpse into what could be.

Consider the way AI analyzes an opponent's strategies and tendencies, offering a detailed playbook for athletes to exploit. It's as if the oracle of Delphi itself were whispering secrets into their ears, guiding them towards victory. This level of insight transforms the way games are played, making every move calculated and purposeful.

AI also serves as an oracle in injury prevention and recovery. By analyzing an athlete's biomechanics and training data, AI can predict the likelihood of injuries and suggest preventive measures. This foresight allows athletes to train smarter, not harder, reducing the risk of career-threatening injuries and prolonging their time in the sport.

The modern-day oracle that is AI offers more than just predictions; it provides a sense of control and confidence to athletes. Knowing that they have the backing of such powerful technology instills a sense of empowerment, allowing them to push their limits and achieve greatness. Just as the oracles of old were pivotal in guiding heroes, AI is indispensable in shaping the champions of today.

5

Chapter 5: Legendary Narratives and Mental Fortitude

The stories of ancient heroes were not just about physical prowess; they were also about mental strength and resilience. Modern athletes, like their mythic counterparts, must possess an unyielding spirit to overcome challenges and achieve greatness. Here, too, AI plays a crucial role in enhancing mental fortitude.

Through virtual reality simulations, athletes can experience high-pressure scenarios that prepare them for real-life competitions. These simulations replicate the intensity and unpredictability of actual games, helping athletes build mental toughness and stay calm under pressure. It's akin to the trials faced by mythic heroes, who had to confront their fears and emerge stronger.

AI also helps athletes develop a winning mindset through personalized psychological training programs. These programs use data to identify mental weaknesses and provide targeted strategies to overcome them. Just as a mythic hero would receive guidance from a wise mentor, modern athletes receive support from AI, enabling them to unlock their full potential.

The fusion of legendary narratives and AI-driven mental training creates a powerful synergy. Athletes are inspired by the tales of old, drawing strength from the heroes who came before them. At the same time, they benefit from the cutting-edge technology that equips them with the mental tools needed to succeed. Together, these elements forge athletes who are not only physically capable but also mentally resilient, ready to take on any challenge that comes their way.

6

Chapter 6: The Role of Myth in Team Dynamics

In ancient myths, heroes often relied on their companions to achieve their quests. Similarly, modern sports teams are built on the foundation of trust, collaboration, and unity. AI has revolutionized the way teams function, fostering a sense of camaraderie and enhancing team dynamics.

Through data analytics, AI provides insights into each team member's strengths and weaknesses, allowing coaches to create strategies that maximize their collective potential. This level of understanding promotes a sense of trust and reliance among team members, much like the bonds formed by mythic heroes and their companions.

AI also enhances communication within teams, enabling real-time feedback and strategic adjustments. This instant flow of information ensures that everyone is on the same page, working together towards a common goal. It's reminiscent of the way mythic heroes would rely on their allies to navigate challenges and achieve their objectives.

Moreover, AI-driven performance analysis helps teams build a culture of continuous improvement. By identifying areas for growth and providing targeted training programs, AI ensures that teams are always striving to be better. This relentless pursuit of excellence is a hallmark of both mythic heroes and modern athletes, driving them to achieve greatness together.

7

Chapter 7: The Ethical Considerations of AI in Sports

The integration of AI in sports raises important ethical questions that must be addressed. Just as mythic heroes grappled with moral dilemmas, modern athletes and organizations must navigate the ethical landscape of AI technology. Issues such as data privacy, fairness, and the potential for misuse are at the forefront of these considerations.

Data privacy is a significant concern, as AI systems rely on vast amounts of personal information to function effectively. Athletes must trust that their data will be handled responsibly and securely. This trust is crucial, as any breach could have serious consequences for their careers and personal lives. Ensuring data privacy is not just a technical challenge but an ethical imperative.

Fairness is another critical issue, as AI has the potential to create disparities in sports. Access to advanced AI technology can give some athletes and teams a competitive edge, leading to questions about equity and fair play. It's essential to ensure that AI benefits are available to all, preventing an uneven playing field that undermines the spirit of competition.

The potential for misuse of AI technology also raises ethical concerns. AI can be used to enhance performance in ways that may be considered unethical or even illegal. Establishing clear guidelines and regulations is necessary to prevent such abuses and maintain the integrity of sports. Just as mythic heroes had to adhere to a code of honor, modern athletes and organizations must uphold ethical standards in their use of AI.

8

Chapter 8: The Future of AI and Myth in Athletics

As AI continues to evolve, its impact on sports will only grow. The future holds exciting possibilities, from advanced predictive models that can foresee entire seasons to AI-driven training programs that adapt in real-time. This ongoing evolution promises to push the boundaries of athletic performance even further, enabling athletes to reach new heights of achievement.

One exciting development is the potential for AI to revolutionize talent scouting. By analyzing vast amounts of data from youth leagues and amateur competitions, AI can identify promising athletes who may have been overlooked. This democratization of talent discovery ensures that everyone has a fair chance to showcase their skills and achieve their dreams.

Additionally, AI could play a crucial role in enhancing fan engagement. Imagine personalized experiences where fans receive real-time updates and insights tailored to their preferences. Virtual reality could bring fans closer to the action than ever before, offering immersive experiences that rival being in the stadium. The myths of old may have been passed down through storytelling, but the legends of tomorrow will be experienced firsthand through cutting-edge technology.

As AI and mythology continue to intertwine, the future of athletics looks brighter than ever. The stories of ancient heroes will continue to inspire, while AI provides the tools and insights needed to achieve greatness. Together, they will shape a new era of sports, where the line between myth and reality becomes increasingly blurred.

9

Chapter 9: The Human Element in an AI-Driven World

Despite the incredible advancements in AI, the human element remains at the heart of athletics. The passion, dedication, and resilience of athletes are qualities that no machine can replicate. AI may provide the tools and insights, but it is the athletes themselves who must put in the hard work and make the sacrifices necessary to succeed.

This human element is what makes sports so compelling. The thrill of victory, the agony of defeat, and the stories of perseverance against all odds resonate deeply with fans. These emotional connections are what elevate sports from mere competition to a source of inspiration and entertainment for millions around the world.

AI can enhance these experiences by providing deeper insights and creating more engaging narratives, but it can never replace the raw emotion and human drama that make sports so captivating. The legendary stories of ancient heroes remind us that it is the human spirit, with all its imperfections and strengths, that truly defines greatness.

10

Chapter 10: AI and the Evolution of Training Techniques

Training techniques have come a long way since the days of ancient Greece, and AI is at the forefront of this evolution. Advanced algorithms analyze an athlete's performance in real-time, offering instant feedback and personalized training plans. This level of precision ensures that every aspect of an athlete's preparation is optimized for success.

One area where AI has made a significant impact is in injury prevention and recovery. By analyzing biomechanical data, AI can identify potential injury risks and recommend corrective measures. This proactive approach helps athletes stay healthy and avoid setbacks that could derail their careers.

AI also plays a crucial role in optimizing nutrition and recovery strategies. Personalized meal plans and recovery protocols ensure that athletes receive the right nutrients and rest to perform at their best. These advancements are transforming the way athletes train and compete, pushing the limits of human potential.

11

Chapter 11: The Power of Myth and AI in Shaping Athletes' Identity

The stories athletes tell themselves about their journey can have a profound impact on their performance. Mythology has long been a source of inspiration, offering powerful narratives that help athletes frame their experiences and overcome challenges. AI, too, can play a role in shaping these narratives, providing data-driven insights that reinforce an athlete's belief in their abilities.

Through AI-driven mental training programs, athletes can develop a strong sense of identity and purpose. Visualization techniques, augmented by AI, help athletes picture themselves achieving their goals and overcoming obstacles. This mental conditioning is crucial for building confidence and resilience, allowing athletes to perform at their peak.

The fusion of myth and AI creates a powerful synergy that empowers athletes to reach new heights. The legendary stories of old provide the inspiration, while AI offers the tools and insights needed to turn those dreams into reality. Together, they shape athletes' identities, guiding them on their quest for greatness.

12

Chapter 12: The Enduring Legacy of Myth and AI in Sports

As we look to the future, it is clear that the legacy of myth and AI in sports will endure. These two seemingly disparate elements have come together to create a new era of athletics, where technology and storytelling work hand in hand to push the boundaries of human potential.

The myths of ancient heroes will continue to inspire, reminding us of the timeless qualities of courage, resilience, and excellence. At the same time, AI will continue to evolve, providing new tools and insights that help athletes achieve their dreams. This enduring legacy will shape the future of sports, ensuring that the spirit of competition and the pursuit of greatness remain at the heart of athletic endeavors.

In the end, the mythic match between AI and legendary stories is not just about technology and data; it is about the human spirit and the quest for excellence. Together, they create a powerful narrative that inspires and drives athletes to achieve greatness, leaving a lasting impact on the world of sports.

13

Chapter 13: AI and the Transformation of Coaching

The role of coaches has been transformed by the integration of AI into athletics. Traditionally, coaches relied on their experience and intuition to guide athletes, but now they have access to a wealth of data and insights that enhance their decision-making. AI provides coaches with detailed analyses of performance, allowing them to tailor training programs to each athlete's specific needs.

This data-driven approach enables coaches to identify areas for improvement and track progress over time. AI-powered tools can analyze video footage, offering insights into technique and form that were previously inaccessible. This level of detail allows coaches to make precise adjustments, optimizing performance and reducing the risk of injury.

Moreover, AI facilitates better communication between coaches and athletes. Real-time feedback and performance metrics ensure that athletes understand their strengths and weaknesses, fostering a collaborative approach to training. This partnership between human intuition and AI-driven insights creates a powerful synergy, enabling coaches to guide athletes to new levels of excellence.

14

Chapter 14: The Impact of AI on Sports Medicine

Sports medicine has been revolutionized by the advent of AI, offering new possibilities for injury prevention, diagnosis, and treatment. AI-driven tools can analyze an athlete's biomechanics, identifying potential risk factors and suggesting corrective measures to prevent injuries before they occur. This proactive approach helps athletes stay healthy and perform at their best.

In the event of an injury, AI can assist in diagnosis and treatment planning. Advanced imaging techniques, combined with AI algorithms, provide detailed insights into the extent of an injury, allowing for more accurate and effective treatment. AI can also monitor an athlete's recovery progress, adjusting rehabilitation programs in real-time to ensure optimal outcomes.

Additionally, AI is transforming the field of personalized medicine. By analyzing an athlete's genetic makeup, AI can provide tailored recommendations for nutrition, training, and recovery. This personalized approach ensures that athletes receive the care and support they need to reach their full potential, paving the way for a new era of sports medicine.

15

Chapter 15: AI and the Evolution of Fan Experience

The fan experience has been dramatically enhanced by the integration of AI into sports. AI-driven platforms provide fans with personalized content, real-time updates, and immersive experiences that bring them closer to the action. From virtual reality broadcasts to interactive statistics, AI is reshaping the way fans engage with their favorite sports.

One of the most exciting developments is the use of AI to create personalized fan experiences. By analyzing user data, AI can recommend content and experiences tailored to each fan's preferences. This level of personalization ensures that fans receive the most relevant and engaging content, enhancing their overall experience.

AI is also transforming the way fans interact with live events. Real-time analytics and interactive features provide fans with deeper insights into the game, allowing them to become more immersed in the action. Virtual reality and augmented reality technologies offer immersive experiences that make fans feel as if they are part of the game, creating unforgettable moments.

16

Chapter 16: The Role of AI in Sports Broadcasting

Sports broadcasting has been revolutionized by the integration of AI, offering new possibilities for coverage and analysis. AI-driven tools can analyze live footage, providing real-time insights and statistics that enhance the viewing experience. This level of detail ensures that fans receive the most comprehensive and engaging coverage possible.

AI also plays a crucial role in content creation and distribution. Automated systems can generate highlights and summaries, ensuring that fans never miss a moment of the action. These AI-generated clips can be distributed across multiple platforms, reaching a wider audience and enhancing fan engagement.

Moreover, AI-driven analytics provide broadcasters with deeper insights into audience preferences and behavior. This data allows broadcasters to tailor their content and delivery strategies, ensuring that they meet the needs of their audience. By combining human expertise with AI-driven insights, sports broadcasters can create a more dynamic and engaging viewing experience.

17

Chapter 17: The Future of AI and Myth in Athletics

As we look to the future, the integration of AI and mythology in athletics will continue to shape the world of sports. The stories of ancient heroes will remain a source of inspiration, guiding athletes in their quests for greatness. At the same time, AI will continue to evolve, offering new tools and insights that push the boundaries of human potential.

One exciting possibility is the development of AI-driven training environments that replicate the challenges faced by mythic heroes. These virtual reality simulations will allow athletes to experience the trials and triumphs of legendary figures, inspiring them to reach new heights. This fusion of myth and technology will create a powerful narrative that motivates and empowers athletes.

As AI continues to advance, its impact on sports will be profound. The stories of ancient heroes will be woven into the fabric of modern athletics, creating a legacy that endures for generations to come. The mythic match between AI and legendary stories will shape the future of sports, ensuring that the pursuit of excellence remains at the heart of athletic endeavors.

Book Description

Step into a world where ancient myths and cutting-edge technology converge to shape the future of sports. In "The Mythic Match: How Artificial

Intelligence and Legendary Stories Shape Modern Athletics," readers are taken on an exhilarating journey through the fascinating intersection of AI and legendary narratives that have defined athletic excellence throughout history.

Explore how artificial intelligence is revolutionizing every aspect of sports, from personalized training regimens to injury prevention and recovery. Discover the incredible ways in which AI serves as a modern-day oracle, offering predictive insights that guide athletes and coaches to victory. Witness the transformation of sports medicine, fan engagement, and broadcasting, all powered by AI's remarkable capabilities.

At the heart of this book lies a deep appreciation for the timeless stories of ancient heroes and their enduring impact on modern athletes. The legendary tales of Achilles, Hercules, and other mythic figures provide a powerful narrative framework that continues to inspire and motivate today's sports stars. Through the fusion of myth and technology, athletes are empowered to unlock their full potential and achieve greatness.

"The Mythic Match" is not just a book about sports; it's a celebration of the human spirit and the relentless pursuit of excellence. Whether you're an athlete, a coach, a sports enthusiast, or simply someone intrigued by the possibilities of AI, this book offers a captivating and insightful look at the future of athletics. Join us on this epic journey and discover how the past and future come together to shape the present in the world of modern sports.